A GIFT FOR:

_____

FROM:

_____

EVERYTHING I NEED TO KNOW I LEARNED FROM PEANUTS

CHARLES M. SCHULZ

GIFT BOOKS

RUNNING PRESS
PHILADELPHIA · LONDON

Happy Birthday, Peanuts!

The year 2010 marks the Diamond Anniversary of Peanuts. Over the years Snoopy has taught us how to live life to the fullest, Lucy has taught us the wisdom of the ages through a unique brand of advanced psychiatry involving nickels, Linus has taught us that security can be found in a soft blue blankie, and we have worked out our worst fears and anxieties through good old Charlie Brown. In reviewing the evolution of Snoopy, Charlie Brown, Lucy, Linus, Peppermint Patty, Marcie, Schroeder, Rerun, and the rest of the gang, it becomes apparent that everything we need to know can be learned from Peanuts. They have given us a "How to" on just about every topic, pearls of wisdom to last a lifetime, and have pointed out what's most important for us. So grab a big slice of birthday cake and settle down to some of the best life lessons, as told by the wisest group of kindergarteners on the planet.

How to get the best seat
in the house . . .

How to become
a golf pro . . .

How to fight back...

LUCY SAID IF I NEED TWENTY-FIVE DOLLARS TO BUY PEGGY JEAN A CHRISTMAS PRESENT, I SHOULD SELL MY DOG...

© 1990 United Feature Syndicate, Inc.

WHAT A GREAT IDEA!

THAT'S THE FIRST TIME I'VE EVER SEEN HIM SPILL HIS WATER DISH..

12/6

SCHULZ

A Pearl of Wisdom from

SNOOPY

I GAVE UP TRYING
TO UNDERSTAND PEOPLE
LONG AGO. NOW I
JUST LET THEM TRY TO
UNDERSTAND ME!

THE IMPORTANCE OF

Knowing When Enough Is Enough

SURE, IT'S ALWAYS ME, ISN'T IT?

ALL RIGHT, IF THAT'S THE WAY EVERYBODY FEELS, I'LL LEAVE!

I KNOW WHEN I'M NOT WANTED! I KNOW WHEN I'M NOT LOVED! I KNOW WHEN EVERYONE IS AGAINST ME!

WHEN?

WHEN?! WHAT DO YOU MEAN, WHEN?!

I MEAN, DID YOU KNOW THE EXACT MOMENT WHEN YOU WEREN'T WANTED, AND NOT LOVED, AND EVERYONE WAS AGAINST YOU?

9-14

OR DID YOU MAYBE HAVE THE FEELING COMING ON LAST WEEK OR LAST MONTH, OR MAYBE...

© 1997 United Feature Syndicate, Inc.

FOR INSTANCE, I KNEW THE EXACT MOMENT WHEN I WAS OVERDOING IT..

How to get to the root
of bible stories . . .

How to make friends...

How to be profound . . .

A Pearl of Wisdom from

CHARLIE BROWN

THE SECRET OF HAPPINESS
IS HAVING THREE THINGS
TO LOOK FORWARD TO, AND
NOTHING TO DREAD!

THE IMPORTANCE OF

Knowing the Rules of the Game

How to earn brownie points
with your teacher...

How to offend
a serious musician . . .

How to shop for
those difficult ones on your
Christmas list . . .

A Pearl of Wisdom from

LUCY

THE WORLD CAN'T COME
TO AN END TODAY
BECAUSE IT IS ALREADY
TOMORROW IN SOME OTHER
PART OF THE WORLD!

THE IMPORTANCE OF

Nature in Solving Life's Problems

How to spend
that post-retirement
spare time . . .

How to be a team leader . . .

How the circle of
life turns...

NEVER SET YOUR STOMACH
FOR A JELLY-BREAD
SANDWICH UNTIL YOU'RE
SURE THERE'S SOME JELLY!

THE IMPORTANCE OF

Perseverance

PEANUTS by Schulz

HERE, YOU GOT SOME MORE LETTERS FROM EDITORS..

DO THEY LIKE MY STORIES?

"DEAR CONTRIBUTOR, WHO TOLD YOU THAT YOU COULD WRITE, YOUR MOTHER?"

"DEAR CONTRIBUTOR, WE'VE SEEN BETTER WRITING ON LICENSE PLATES.."

"DEAR CONTRIBUTOR, IF YOU SEND US ANY MORE STORIES, WE'RE COMING TO YOUR HOUSE AND PUNCH YOU OUT!"

"DEAR CONTRIBUTOR, IF YOU SEND US ONE MORE DUMB STORY, WE'RE GOING TO HAVE TO NAIL OUR MAILBOX SHUT!"

I FILED THEM WITH ALL THE OTHERS..

1-26

How to be tactful . . .

How to win a girl's heart...

How to make up excuses
for skipping class . . .

A Pearl of Wisdom from

PEPPERMINT PATTY

NEVER GIVE YOUR HEART
TO A BLOCKHEAD.

THE IMPORTANCE OF

Technology

How to be a success...

How to cope when you've forgotten your umbrella...

How to recharge after a workout…

A Pearl of Wisdom from

PIGPEN

THE WORLD NEEDS
MESSY PEOPLE . . .
OTHERWISE THE NEAT
PEOPLE WOULD TAKE OVER!

THE IMPORTANCE OF

Having a Good Attorney

How to get a free meal . . .

How to listen
to your body . . .

How to accept
constructive criticism . . .

SALLY

WHO CARES WHAT OTHER PEOPLE THINK?

THE IMPORTANCE OF

Having the Right Answers

PEANUTS by Schulz

WHAT WE NEED IS CONFIDENCE!

ASK YOURSELF THE QUESTION, "CAN WE WIN?" THEN, SAY, "YES, WE'RE GONNA WIN!"

"CAN WE WIN?" "HA! FORGET IT! NO WAY! NOT IN A MILLION YEARS!"

3-24

HEY, MANAGER.. I GOT SOME ANSWERS, BUT I DON'T THINK YOU'RE GONNA LIKE 'EM..

TAKE HER AWAY! SOMEBODY GET HER OUT OF HERE! SHE'S GONNA DRIVE ME CRAZY!!

HEY, MANAGER.. TELL ME AGAIN.. WHAT WAS THE QUESTION?

How to learn from our elders...

How to have
a good conversation . . .

How to get a guy . . .

A Pearl of Wisdom from

THE FLYING ACE

ITS EITHER THE FLU
OR LOVE ... THE SYMPTOMS
ARE THE SAME.

THE IMPORTANCE OF

Having a Dog

PEANUTS by SCHULZ

SOMETIMES I LIE AWAKE AT NIGHT, AND I THINK..

..OR I SORT OF ASK..

I MEAN, I LIE HERE IN THE DARK, AND..

WOOF!

OR ELSE, I JUST LIE AWAKE, AND I WONDER, OR..

© 1996 United Feature Syndicate, Inc.

..OR I ASK..

AND THEN THIS VOICE COMES TO ME THAT SAYS..

"YOU HAVE A DOG..BE HAPPY!"

3-31

How to know when
a relationship is
going nowhere . . .

How to bargain . . .

How to get famous . . .

A Pearl of Wisdom from

MARCIE

WAKE UP AND SMELL
THE BUBBLE GUM.

THE IMPORTANCE OF

Humility

How to deal
with censorship . . .

How to shut people up . . .

How to eat ice cream . . .

A Pearl of Wisdom from

RERUN

I'VE LEARNED ALL
I NEED TO KNOW TO LIVE
UNDER A BED.

THE IMPORTANCE OF

Making Yourself at Home

OKAY, TROOPS, HERE'S WHERE WE'LL SPEND THE NIGHT..

I'LL GO OFF AND GATHER SOME FIREWOOD WHILE YOU PREPARE THE CAMP

WE'RE GOING TO BE HERE FOR A COUPLE OF DAYS SO MAKE IT A HAPPY PLACE..

How to appear intelligent . . .

How to avoid
difficult questions . . .

How to make a person
uncomfortable . . .

A Pearl of Wisdom from

SCHROEDER

———————

TO ME, LOVE SONGS
ARE LIKE EATING
TOO MUCH ICE CREAM.

THE IMPORTANCE OF

Helping a Friend ... Or at Least Trying to

YES, SIR..A RED ONE..

WHAT? YOU'RE KIDDING!

THEY WON'T SELL ME A KITE.. THEY SAY I'LL JUST GET IT CAUGHT IN A TREE..

THEY SAY I'M GIVING KITE FLYING A BAD NAME..

THAT'S RIDICULOUS! GIVE ME YOUR MONEY..I'LL GO BUY IT FOR YOU..

YES, SIR..I WANT TO BUY A RED KITE..

OF COURSE, IT'S FOR MYSELF! WHAT DID YOU THINK I WAS GOING TO DO..GIVE IT TO MY FRIEND, CHARLIE BROWN?!

3-10

HERE, I BOUGHT YOU A MARBLE..

How to get work done
in a pinch . . .

How to find security . . .

How to fake it . . .

A Pearl of Wisdom from

JOE COOL

ACTUALLY, WE JOE
COOLS ARE SCARED TO
DEATH OF CHICKS.

THE IMPORTANCE OF

Good Sportsmanship

C'MON, CHARLIE BROWN...STRIKE OUT THE FAT KID!

THAT'S OKAY.. LET'S GET THE SKINNY KID!

HEY, CEMENT HEAD! WHO SAID YOU COULD HIT?!

HEY, NOODLE NECK! YOU SWING LIKE MY GRANDMOTHER!

WELL, WE LOST AGAIN.. BY THE WAY, SOME OF THEIR PLAYERS WANT TO TALK TO YOU..

PLAYERS? WHAT PLAYERS?

THE FAT KID, THE SKINNY KID, CEMENT HEAD, AND NOODLE NECK..

I THINK I'LL GO HOME A DIFFERENT WAY..

7-13

How to tell a turtle
from a hubcap...

IF YOU HAVE ENJOYED THIS BOOK, WE WOULD LOVE TO HEAR FROM YOU.

PLEASE SEND YOUR COMMENTS TO:

Hallmark Book Feedback
P.O. Box 419034
Mail Drop 215
Kansas City, MO 64141

OR E-MAIL US AT:

booknotes@hallmark.com